CONFRONTING AN EXTRATERRESTRIAL

CONFRONTING AN EXTRATERRESTRIAL

Six Precautions You Must Take

Claude Joseph

Library of Congress Control Number:		2017912484
ISBN:	Hardcover	978-1-5434-0273-5
	Softcover	978-1-5434-0272-8
	eBook	978-1-5434-0271-1

Print information available on the last page.

To order additional copies of this book, contact:
Xlibris
1-800-455-039
www.Xlibris.com.au
Orders@Xlibris.com.au
761544

For Janine Joseph

Earlier books by Claude Joseph:

Cape Paterson

The Milk Run

The Robotoid Spy

Another Being

This is the fictional reference book referred to in the story
Another Being.

CONTENTS

Prologue

Do you have an appointment or are you expecting to catch an extraterrestrial by surprise?

Either way, I can see that you are an overachiever when it comes to reaching out to different cultures. Confronting an extraterrestrial will stretch your social skills, emotional intelligence, and tolerance to the limit. It won't just be a personal achievement; it will be a history-making one. You will be representing all of us here on Earth.

Important note: That bright light you saw in the sky may have been ball lightning. Oh, and that saucer shape could have been a lenticular cloud. The short grey being with bulging oval head, slanted eye slits, and spindly legs you saw rush out of the convenience store at midnight may have been a juvenile robber wearing an oversized grey beanie with eye slits cut at the wrong angle. So, don't get your hopes too high if that's all you saw.

But at least you are preparing for a first contact. When I had my first contact, I didn't recognise it as such.

In fact, I was launching my dog-wash business. The constant whirr of my roof wind turbines could be heard as a warm summer breeze swept through. Driverless vehicles arrived at allotted times with their scruffy-looking hounds poking their snouts out the side window, tongues hanging. I was farewelling a bathed basset when a driverless stretch limousine rolled up my drive-through. Inside was Puffy Lace's dachshund. Puffy was a pop star who lived only three blocks away. I was chuffed when she had booked her pooch in.

Suddenly sports cars and motorbikes pulled up in the street at all angles. The paparazzi took their positions at my front gate, extending the zoom lenses of their cameras. They focused on the limousine while I opened its middle door. But when they saw only a long-bodied dog emerge from the limo, their hopes were dashed. They started to pack up their cameras and walk away. The cameramen had no interest in my business launch or a celebrity's dog. They were hoping to see Puffy in person.

It was at that moment a tumultuous roar emanated from the sky. A wedge-shaped spacecraft cut through a cloud and screeched downward in our direction. It was hell-bent on gatecrashing the opening day of my new business venture. It skidded on my manicured lawn, finally coming to rest in the front garden. Excess rocket propellant was spewing out of its exhaust vents.

Everyone stared for a few moments. A dog flap pushed out. To our amazement, a four-legged, bear-sized creature staggered through. Its front paws lurched forward and its hind legs splayed suddenly as if doing the splits. Still adjusting to Earth's gravity, it drew its space legs into a more load-bearing gait. A camera clasped its forehead, a light-blue costume with circular motifs of stars and planets hugged its body, and an orange metallic band hung firmly around its neck like a collar. It sniffed the air as if traces of its favourite smell were present. Maybe it was my potting mix.

I just gawked until I realised the paparazzi were expecting me to wash the bear-like dog. I approached the dog at an angle, suavely. I slotted my hands into my pockets and pretended to focus on my gumboots. I began a faint whistle, I wanted to mollify the dog not rile it up. The dog looked at me, eyes attentive and wary, ears pricked.

The press went wild. I couldn't ask for better publicity than that. Now they were interested in my dog wash. Now they had a story. The publicity was bound to be more effective than the finger-printed message on the deliberately dirty rear window of my car saying, 'If you think this window needs a clean, your dog needs one more, ring Claude's Dog Wash today.'

'You can come in,' I called out. 'I'm launching my dog-wash business today.'

One cameraman unlatched my gate and strolled through my front garden, intrigued.

'You have some high-rolling customers, I can see,' he noted.

I nodded. The fact of the matter was I had no idea what just happened, but I was determined to make the most of it.

● ● ●

I hope you have some idea of what sort of manifestation of an extraterrestrial you are expecting to confront. It might not even have a front or back. It could well be a featureless mass of writhing organic gelatine. Or, it could have a scarier face than any ghoul you have seen on Halloween. Brace for it! You could be on a ride of a lifetime, facing your deepest fears and crossing the threshold into the unknown.

The extraterrestrial may even be a robot. It is far more likely that a robot would visit our planet than a biological being. A robot would be able to withstand the gamma rays in space and the vast amount of time the journey would take. It wouldn't need any food, water, or oxygen.

Whatever body form the extraterrestrial may take, the following are general precautions you should take to avoid putting yourself at risk. If you are unable to take these precautions, you should strongly reconsider confronting an extraterrestrial at all.

Precaution 1

Have GovSnoop Authority

1.1 GovSnoop introduction

GovSnoop are the government, and they are used to getting their own way. You know they like to snoop into everybody's business. So, no matter how intrusive they get, never say to them, 'None of your business.' Everything is their business. Their motto is 'Tell us, or hear from us.' Don't think you can fob them off. They have a habit of pulling up in your driveway in their black SUVs at the most inconvenient time. Like when you're in the shower minutes before your taxicab is due to rush you off to the airport to make the last flight that will get you to your sister's wedding in time. They have tools to wipe out forbidden memories from some people and sharpen forgotten memories of others.

You know they probably have their cameras trained on you right now. I didn't ask you to look behind; now you've shown your face.

I bet you think they are hiding aliens, but they think you are. Extraterrestrial encounters are a tricky, twisted business; you need to tread carefully.

I would avoid letting people see you reading this book especially if you haven't contacted GovSnoop yet. I wouldn't read it on public transport; you never know who is sitting behind you. You're not on a bus now, are you?

Better to leave no record of ever having read this book. If you borrowed it from a public library, cancel your library card after you return it and request a new one. Borrow something down to earth like *The Earth Moved: On the Remarkable Achievements of Earthworms*.[1] It is one thing to be reading about giant Gippsland[2] earthworms. It's quite another to be reading about what's necessary to fend off giant Alpha Centaurians reaching Earth via a wormhole.

So, who should you see in GovSnoop? I can tell you—not the officers in Area 51.[3] The waiting white SUV[4] on the hilltop will scream down and apprehend you before you can say, 'I saw a

---

[1] A. Stewart, *The Earth Moved: On the Remarkable Achievements of Earthworms*, first paperback edn., Chapel Hill, NC, Algonquin Books, 2005, pp. 116-120.

[2] Gippsland is in south-eastern Victoria, Australia.

[3] Site of US air force base in Nevada that tests advanced aircraft and is claimed to have held an alien wreck

[4] A sport utility vehicle capable of use off-road

UFO.'[5] You'll be slapped with a $1,000 fine, a day in court, and a possible lifetime ban on entering the US.[6]

You'll be much better off seeing the GovSnoop director in Washington DC, the one whose office has a hidden entrance into a chamber full of extraterrestrial artefacts. At least he's not going to say, 'Poppycock.' I heard he keeps a world globe as big as the Times Square ball in the chamber. It is speckled with labels revealing locations of confirmed UFO sightings. He'll be only too pleased to pop a sticker on for your encounter.

Or if that's out of your way, you can always ring their contact centre number. At least you'll be given a case number to prove you contacted them.

1.2 Making your case

Prepare a speech on why you think you should be the one to make first contact. For instance, how you have a master's degree in Communications at UCLA[7] and a PhD in Psychology at Rice University, Texas. Share with them your experience living amongst Navajo Native Americans on their reservation. Recount the training the Navajo gave you on tracking creatures and surviving

---

[5] Unidentified flying object

[6] This happened to an Adventure Photo Tours Inc. driver.

[7] University of California, Los Angeles

long periods without water. Identify the cacti that you can tap juice from as an alternative to bottled water.

How did you go in high school arithmetic? You'll need to brush up on your maths, especially the prime numbers and Pythagoras' theorem. Use a maths primer if you need to. Mathematical relationships are universal, pre-existing any discovery. They are also unambiguous. A dim-witted-looking extraterrestrial could use them to prove to you that it is smart. Or it could test you! So GovSnoop will be reassured that you have some level of competence if you show them your Maths Challenge certificate.

Musical melodies are also universal, pre-existing any discovery. A short interlude during your encounter will help break the ice. But if you sing opera, don't overdo it; it may break the glass windows of the alien's spaceship too! A culturally refined extraterrestrial may repeat a series of notes to you. Play your flute to GovSnoop so that they know you will be able to respond in kind.

Tell them how you persevered training your parrot or goldfish no matter how moronically it responded. All relevant experience counts!

Show them your birth certificate so that there is no question that you are an American citizen. They want to know that should you be asked to take the extraterrestrial to your leader, you'll take it to the United States president, not the sombrero-wearing Mexican one.

Furthermore, GovSnoop want to know that when you tell the extraterrestrial the name of our planet, you'll use the English name, Earth, not the French name, Terre. The first name it hears is what will stick.

On that subject, history has shown that explorers have repeatedly mispronounced native place names and those mispronunciations have stuck. Take *Alaska* for example. It came from the corruption of the Aleut[8] word *Alaxsxa* meaning mainland. The word *Earth* is particularly susceptible to sounding like a burp. So, don't belch when you say it, otherwise the rest of the galaxy may end up making embarrassing sounds whenever they refer to our planet.

Alternatively, you may suggest confronting the extraterrestrial together. Convince GovSnoop that only you can figure out where the extraterrestrial is likely to be. By GovSnoop accompanying you, their authorisation is implicit. That's what I did when an alien creature descended on me. As it turned out, that was the best precaution I took.

Before you contact them, make sure your taxes are in order, you don't have any outstanding parking fines, and you haven't tried to enter Area 51 without permission. Oh, and remember to duly return that book *The Earth Moved: On the Remarkable Achievements of Earthworms* that I suggested you borrow.

---

[8] Native people of the western portion of the Alaska Peninsula, in south-western Alaska extending to the Pacific Ocean and the Aleutian Islands

1.3 Personal case study

After entering every digit in turn on their IVR[9] system, my conversation with a real GovSnoop woman went something like this:

'Congratulations, you're the first caller this year who hasn't had his or her call routed down one of our self-serve selections, and believe me, we have one for every conceivable call reason,' announced the woman using what I presumed to be her pristine-condition desk phone.

'Well, perhaps that's because I have no ordinary matter to report,' I said. I was trying my hardest to contain my excitement.

'Shoot,' she said in a flat tone.

'We have been visited,' I fired back.

'Pardon,' she said, making a crunching sound that I imagined to be a celery stick being bitten off.

'Extraterrestrial, no less,' I said.

'If you think I am going to believe a crank caller who has watched *Ancient Aliens*[10] a few too many times, you are mistaken. Prank or crank, I am not here to listen to nonsense.'

'This is nothing like that. I wouldn't dream of wasting your time.' I said sweetly. 'I've got an actual spacecraft to show for, and more. I'd like to book an appointment with GovSnoop, onsite.'

---

[9] Interactive voice response

[10] An American television series about aliens having visited Earth

She sighed, 'You are aware of the penalties if this turns out to be a hoax, aren't you?'

'Yes, six months in a cool room, shovelling ice.'

'You do know your governmental policy.' I could tell she was impressed.

I have to admit I sweated that the spacecraft could vanish in the meantime, but at least I had media witnesses and video recordings.

'In view of the gravity of your claim, two of my agents will meet you at 9:00 a.m. tomorrow. Just enter the address on your keypad.'

'There,' I said as I pressed the Send button.

'That's your house,' she said after some time searching the GovSnoop high-definition photographic database. 'You should give me the name of your landscape gardener, there isn't a blade of grass out of place.' She panned to the right. 'Must get a lot of visitors with a drive-through like that.' She thumbed to the house and noticed the thick curtains on all the front-facing windows. My privacy-loving wife had drawn them all when she had seen the GovSnoop van coming around last week to photograph the house. My wife, Veronica, didn't want them to be peeping inside the house, especially as the beds hadn't been made yet. 'Have you been harbouring the alien behind the curtains?'

'No, it sleeps in its spacecraft.' What was she thinking, that I adopted it and furnished it with its own bedroom? I felt peeved that she would think that of me. The spacecraft only just arrived. It wasn't even there at the time GovSnoop photographed my house.

'You wash dogs?' she quizzed as if the huge neon sign out the front wasn't convincing enough.

'Just starting up my own business,' I replied.

Losing interest, she asked, 'Is there anything else I can help you with?'

'No, that will be all.'

'Just hang on a second while my computer spits out your case number. Have you got a pen ready?'

'Yes.'

'Case number 232273385. If you need to contact us again, quote that UFO case number.' She hung up the phone.

Precaution 2

Be Armed

2.1 Fit-out

Whether you use bullets, arrows, hand grenades, pepper spray, or your own body odour, you need to be armed. It's not only your constitutional right,[11] your life may depend on it.

You should also consider defensive measures like wearing multipurpose contamination headgear, even if it makes your head look like a cylinder block. You don't know what disease-causing microorganisms the extraterrestrial could be harbouring. Perhaps its spacecraft reactor leaks harmful radiation.

Wear a bulletproof vest, body armour, or exoskeleton. A side benefit is that you'll look tougher.

---

[11] The Second Amendment states that the right of the people to keep and bear arms shall not be infringed.

Wear earmuffs in case it switches on its sonic wave gun.

Wear good running shoes in case you need to chase it or it chases you. Spiked soles could be handy in case you need to kick it in the head. If the alien doesn't seem to have a head, kick it somewhere else that will hurt, like the eyestalk or the lower body.

However, be careful not to touch the alien with your bare skin, especially if you have a cut or open wound. Its body could secrete a toxic substance like a poison dart frog. In any case, wear mittens.

Doors are the most annoying obstacle during a chase. In the tool kit in your black attaché case, carry a battery-powered laser cutter to open doors and a battery-powered welder to seal them.

Bring a waterproof satellite phone so that you can always call home or call for help. Carry a torch too.

How should you dress? I hear you ask. Formal or informal? Should you wear camouflage like army fatigues or should you stand out in a fluorescent safety vest like a road worker? Neither— dress like an ambassador. You're the first person it will see, so make us look good.

Make sure those slim-fit black cargo pants have deep pockets where you can conceal a gun and two magazines of ammunition. Throw in a pocketknife in case you get tied up.

To supply yourself with arms, may I suggest the firearms shop in Vero Beach, Florida. They have dart guns there. The owner used them to bring down marauding brown bears. That should be your first choice because if you end up being hauled up before an alien war crimes tribunal, you can at least claim you didn't intend any harm. In case you live in the Old World, Third World, or down under, they deliver worldwide. Just ensure you empty the magazine in case of returns. We don't want anybody to be shot from a delivery drone knocked about by bad weather.

In case you end up finding yourself in hand-to-paw combat with the creature, it would help if you were trained in kung fu.[12] It will be more effective against extraterrestrials because they are unlikely to have knowledge of those moves. It's not like they would have gone to kung fu classes themselves and learned how to counteract them. But if the creature is bigger and stronger, the use of speed, agility, and technique will help you only so far. There is a threshold beyond which no amount of these fighting styles will help. In that case, arm yourself, or run.

2.2 Planning

Any alien creature is likely to have evolved from a hunter-or-hunted past. That doesn't lend itself to merciful traits. You need to have a plan and, in case that doesn't work, an exit strategy.

The plan should include the rendezvous point, the time, and the duration you limit yourself to. Avoid locations near airports and power transmission lines. Wait for clear weather. You don't want anything to distract you from this once-in-a-lifetime encounter.

The exit strategy should include go-no-go checkpoints, fall back procedure, and contact numbers. If you are getting too

---

[12] Chinese martial arts

close to nightfall, you should pull out. You should prepare to eject yourself out of harm's way at a moment's notice. I would suggest carrying a jet pack. Run through a dress rehearsal of these procedures with your companions.

Lodge your plan and exit strategy with GovSnoop and share a copy with your next of kin. GovSnoop doesn't want to be conducting a missing-persons search prematurely.

You will need to take identification as you don't know where the extraterrestrial may lead you. It may whisk you into its spacecraft for a quick examination and then jettison you in another country.

I would take your passport and drivers licence. Now I don't mean the Martian passport you got at the Martian Embassy[13] in Sydney, Australia. That's only good for travel between Earth and Mars and limits you to one ray gun. Nor do I mean the UFO license you got at the Little A'Le'Inn in Rachel, Nevada. You're not the stated 3 foot 3 inches in height. I mean your very own passport and driver's licence. There is nothing worse than being in a foreign country without proper documentation. As an illegal alien in that country, you will be treated with more suspicion and less humanity than any spacefaring extraterrestrial would imagine treating you.

---

[13] The Martian Embassy in Redfern, part of the Sydney Story Factory, encourages creative writing by indigenous, marginalised, and non-English-speaking-background youth.

2.3 The confrontation

Once in the field, if you see a ray gun being gradually lowered in the direction of your head, immediately fall forward on one knee as an experienced soldier would. That will allow you to reposition for attack.

If you can get close without having a ray gun pointed at you, hold your stance and face the alien squarely. You want to establish your authority. Show poise and dignity. Let it fumble about.

If its handkerchief falls, don't pick it up. This is not the time to be courteous. Apart from having disgusting germs from one of its mucous orifices, you don't want to bend over. That would put you in a vulnerable position.

It may be hard to disable an alien in one strike. Its critical body functions may be redundantly distributed; it could have four hearts and two brains. It may be able to regenerate organs. The second you shoot a lung, a new one might puff up into its place! It could have a false eye. You may be aiming at its bottom. So, you better think twice about ignoring Precaution 5: Demonstrate Goodwill. If you don't take it out in one go, you will have declared yourself to be hostile, and a bad shooter.

Size up your opponent's physique. If it is rotund, it will probably bowl over trying to catch up with you. But if it is brawny, you may have to give it the slip when it reaches over to wallop you.

Determine whether the extraterrestrial is a juvenile or an adult. You may have the courage to confront a similar-sized being to yourself, but what if the creature you spotted was only a child and their protective parent, a costume-busting hulk, is coming up behind? The quickest way to find out is to get a glimpse of the door of its spaceship. If the being is more than three-quarters the height of the door, you may safely assume it is an adult.

What if the alien's spaceship is out of sight? In that case, look for playful behaviour. If it is seeing how high its ball bounces, it is bound to be a kid.

Size up your opponent's weaponry. Refrain from confronting it further unless you can match its array of weapons. Your opponent may be concealing weapons. So, assume any attachment or standalone object whose function is unknown could house a weapon.

Armaments should only be used as a last resort. As I mentioned before, you don't want to appear hostile from the outset. Please use any weapon in moderation. You don't want to put all of humanity in jeopardy by prompting retaliation. Hey, they could come after me!

If you have to disable its spaceship, get your hands on an army disposal bazooka. Aim for the bottom to tear into its propulsion system. That will stop it terrorising the neighbourhood.

To disable the alien momentarily, fire an electro blast gun. The electric shock will give you enough time to get away.

But if things do get out of hand, you may want to call the Space & Missile Systems Center,[14] El Segundo, Los Angeles, so

---

[14] A subordinate unit of Air Force Space Command, near Los Angeles Air Force Base

keep their phone number handy. They'll put a contract out to shoot down that spaceship that's troubling you. Uncle Sam[15] is always there to lend a hand grenade.

The extraterrestrials would be more technologically advanced than us, having designed a spaceship that could reach Earth from another star system. However, all they have at their disposal is their spaceship. We have the home ground advantage. It's not the fans cheering us on that will make the difference but the developed resources of a planet that we are adapted to.

What if you can sense an alien presence but have never laid eyes on any unworldly being? Like at dawn you notice that all the grass in your backyard is bolt upright. The only way to deal with that situation is to set traps of various sizes in the field of impact. Oh, and use watermelon as bait.

2.4 Personal case study

I had no choice approaching the space dog unarmed. I couldn't let the media see me threaten a client's dog. It was the most hideous junkyard-looking dog I have ever seen. It sat on its haunches, growling and gritting its teeth at me. Its serrated teeth

---

[15] Uncle Sam is a personification of the United States government, having represented the military in their army recruitment posters. The patriotic portrayal is believed to be Sam Wilson, who provided barrels of beef to the US Army during the War of 1812.

were intimidating. When I took a step sideways, it turned its head in my direction instead of moving its gaze.

Suddenly, it charged forward. I quickly turned around showing it my back which I regret now. I felt it lunge at me, shredding my white business shirt. Thankfully, Puffy's dachshund interceded, barking incessantly in a stand-off with the space dog. For a short, elongated dog, it had a lot of fight in it. I decided to give the fearless dachshund an extra rinse for its efforts.

I offered the space dog some of last night's meat loaf. While it was devouring that, I donned my gloves and put the dachshund in one of the sinks and hosed it all over.

Once the space dog abandoned its vicious glare and tense stance, I approached it. I carefully peeled off its jumpsuit, wondering who would put such plush livery on an old mutt. I could see its fur was silver beige all over. I searched for a washing instruction label, but there wasn't one.

The camera crew cheered when I carried the heavy animal into an adjoining large sink, demonstrating that I was able to handle ferocious dogs with the same care as placid dogs. I hosed it all over just like I did for the dachshund.

The two dogs initially glared at each other, both seeming to want to convey their own self-importance, but they relaxed once I started washing them.

I put the jet-setting dog's costume in my personal washing machine and then dryer. The camera crew took keen interest in the extra service I afforded the dog. I felt like I was in a set for a laundry detergent commercial.

After I gave the dachshund its second rinse, the camera crew filmed me leading it back to the limo, which drove off. Then they filmed me leading the unusual dog back to its spacecraft and through its dog flap. They just stood there, watching and waiting. They were hoping the driverless spaceship would then depart so that they could zoom out with that scene. Losing patience, they turned back to my humble advertising sign, 'Claude's Dog Wash', and zoomed out from that. I thought that brand reinforcement was a good way to close.

A photographer for *Women's Circle* magazine approached me.

'Now can you tell us who the high-rolling dog owner is?' asked the cameraman in a pale-pink suit.

'Puffy Lace,' I answered.

'Not the limo client, the spacecraft client,' he clarified.

'I . . . I . . .' I stuttered.

'Client confidentiality,' interceded another cameraman, to my relief.

To tell you the truth, I was hoping they knew. They're supposed to know the habits and idiosyncrasies of every celebrity. I wanted so much for it to be a celebrity's dog because the alternative was that it was from another . . . planet. The thought of an alien arrival gave me an intense bout of the heebie-jeebies.

I watched the media depart, returning the avenue to its backstreet calm. Then I remembered the spacecraft hadn't flown off.

Now I could arm myself. I grabbed my whipper snipper[16] from the garage and marched to the spacecraft. I put my head to the ground and, with an authoritarian tone of voice, called to the dog through its flap. It came out whining meekly, so I let it wander around the front garden while I held the whipper snipper ready to strike.

Despite my conviction of the importance of safety with extraterrestrials, I had to admit that the dog was less likely to be a threat than some other feisty dogs I have come across, so I put the snipper down. Still, I kept a watchful eye on it while I pruned my roses.

I set my small autonomous lawnmower to trim the lawn along the calculated shortest route. The space dog followed at some distance, invigorated by the scent of freshly cut grass.

I was distracted by the space dog flicking its ear in quick succession. I started counting the number of flicks each time to see if they summed to prime numbers. That was until I saw a fly bugging its ear. Alas, they were only involuntary reactions, not a top dog showing off its mathematical mastery.

My largest flower bed was shaped in the form of dog. I had spent weeks perfecting it, planting black petunias for its eyes. I thought it would add a special touch to my dog wash for those who noticed it. Seeing that the space dog was about to trample over my prize azaleas, I chased it off with my whipper snipper that I powered on for extra effect. It was enough that its spacecraft had

---

[16] Also known as a line trimmer

ruined a portion of my lawn. I corralled it down the side garden, where it brushed against a towel hanging from my solar-seeking clothesline. It had automatically rotated so that its line would face towards the sun.

The bounce in its gait when it saw my children's sandpit in the backyard was of instant joy. It proceeded to make waste of the handwashing I had given it. Before long, I saw it performing somersaults in the sand. It was one way of massaging itself from head to bottom in one swift movement. Perhaps I should have given it a flea treatment after the wash because it seemed to be soothing itchy bites. Now it had a coating of sand.

Precaution 3

Wear a Hands-Free Video-Streaming Camera

3.1 Camera introduction

Have you seen how commandos raid a site? You need to reconnoitre the danger safely, and quickly, like they do.

A multi-lens ball-shaped video camera should be worn around your neck. The multiple lenses and microphones will record all around in case you need to toss it into a field of danger. You'll get a sneak view of what is lurking ahead, enabling you to take preventative action. Keep it constantly on so nothing is missed. Don't skimp on cost; this isn't a carrot that you're buying. It needs to be robust enough to withstand being tossed on rock, mud, or snow.

You may notice things in the footage that you didn't see at the time, like the tentacles of the extraterrestrial stealing your GPS[17] device that you've been looking for over the past six months. More importantly, you may record some of their advanced designs. SpaceBiz[18] and GovSnoop will be forever grateful.

But alas, we have come to some unpleasant provisions. A video record is vital should you not survive. As small a consolation as this may be, at least GovSnoop will be able to view what happened to you and break it to your family. They will be warned of the pitfalls that may beset future encounters.

3.2 Camera operation

Use a short cord around your neck; otherwise, the camera would sit too low on your chest. You don't want to take pictures of the alien's feet. Nor should you attach the camera to a helmet, like a coal miner's torch. You might end up filming mere tips of the alien's wispy hair.

Set the camera to wide-angle viewing to cater for a range of heights and girths.

Don't use the flash or strobe on your camera. The extraterrestrial may not take kindly to the dazzling light especially at night-time

---

[17] Global Positioning System

[18] Used to be called NASA, but to emphasise that every project from now on had to have a positive business case, the name was changed to SpaceBiz.

when it can be temporarily blinding. All photography should be discreet.

Make sure you use high-capacity batteries and carry spares. You never know how long your encounter may end up being. The alien creature may communicate slowly like a whale or it may have a lot to get off its chest. After all, if it had travelled alone, you would be the first sentient creature it could express itself to since it departed its planet years earlier. Remember, you might be involved in a chase which could take hours, draining your batteries.

Since you and the camera may not make it back, you must ensure the camera is constantly streaming to a remote computer that someone you trust can access. Please ring that person to confirm that the data is being saved. Don't make my mistake and just assume.

Ensure date and time recording on the camera is enabled. When compared with the computer date and time, this will reveal any time-dilation effects that you may be experiencing. If, God forbid, you end up in their spacecraft, it would be handy to know whether you travelled at near light speed and back.

Admittedly, when the recording is played back, it will look a bit amateurish, not being focussed on anything in particular, but we're not producing a Hollywood movie here. We don't want to see the birthmarks on a glamorous starlet or a tycoon's catamaran sailing into the sunset. Think of it being used as evidence in a crime scene investigation. We're more interested in seeing what harm the alien inflicted.

Ensure the camera also records into the infrared and ultraviolet parts of the spectrum. An alien life form may have evolved to be better seen and understood in one of those bands. It may have markings on its skin or fur which only show up in infrared or ultraviolet. The markings could highlight a sensory organ that you didn't notice or they could vary with the age and gender of the life form. The infrared will especially help at night-time to pick up body heat.

Lastly, you may want to annotate your video clips, so fasten to your pocket a space pen[19] that writes upside down. You never know what position you may end up in, especially if you find yourself in its spacecraft in zero gravity.

3.3 Personal case study

I have found that keeping a video camera recording at all times solves a lot of life's miscommunication mysteries so you don't later have doubts about what you or someone else said. When you momentarily zone out to think about the stranger you kissed at midnight on New Year's Eve and miss the present conversation, you can play it back. It is also excellent for helping to remember and match names and faces. So, I already had my video camera

---

[19] In 1965, Paul C. Fisher invented a ballpoint space pen used by NASA that can write upside down without leaking. When pressure is applied to the ball, the agitated gel-like ink within turns to liquid and flows freely.

running during my dog-wash launch in case I wanted to follow up on a potential client who dropped by to check out my facility.

Because I bought a waterproof model, it withstood all the splashing from the dogs. I was able to play back video footage which revealed patterns in the space dog's behaviour. I noticed that it turned its head in time with my movement, facing me at all times. While I recorded video footage of the mutt, it seemed to be taking footage of me. My hunch was that the space dog was trained as a spy dog.

During the sweltering day when the back door was left open, it scampered through all the rooms in my house, searching for something. The next thing I knew, near Veronica's garden gnome lay a neat pile of memory plugs in a pot. A bowerbird would have been proud of the different colours and shapes in its collection. I wasn't too concerned. Those memory plugs only contained funny cat videos that I had downloaded from the Internet. The only one I would miss was one of an attempt to wash a cat but I could easily download it again.

However, my video recording of this space dog was priceless. I needed it as proof; otherwise everyone will think I am a crackpot. Boy, did the recording help get the zookeeper's attention.

Precaution 4

Never Be Alone

4.1 Need for a companion

If anything, the company will be good, especially if they are as good-looking as my local zookeeper.

There's nothing like the comfort of standing beside a familiar human being when you are faced with a hideous-looking creature. Having somebody to smirk at when the alien you are both confronting exhibits some disgusting behaviour will give you release—for example, when the alien flicks its guts out of its mouth, enwraps a grub it wants to digest, and then sucks its distended stomach back up.

Moreover, a companion will allow you to seek validation from a like-minded person about what you are witnessing. That will ease you into adjusting or possibly overhauling your world view[20]—for example, when your companion assures you, 'A slime mould can be an astronaut.'

Another person is as good as a hands-free video-streaming camera for providing another memory of the experience, another eyewitness who won't shatter on impact and wipe its memory if dropped from three feet.

Unlike an extraterrestrial with eyes all around, we humans have a front and back. It would be good to have someone cover that back of yours. You don't want an extraterrestrial to come up from behind and put the wind up you. You'll be shaking in your boots. You want your companion to spot them first and blast them with liquid nitrogen, cold burning them on contact with the rapidly freezing fluid.

The most important reason you should never be alone is if you get injured. You'll certainly want there to be somebody who will come to your aid, bandage you up, and carry you away on a stretcher. While on that subject, make sure your first aid kit has been replenished.

---

[20] A. Harrison, 'Encountering extraterrestrial intelligence', *The Psychologist*, vol. 28, no. 10, October 2015, p. 818.

4.2 Companion selection

Now I'm not expecting you to search an online dating website. This is about teamwork, not love interest. We're not interested in whether your chosen companion enjoys evening strolls along the beach; we want to know whether he or she can hold the beachhead.

Choose someone to accompany you who has a mild temperament. You want someone who will help control the situation and guide the encounter to a fruitful and peaceful conclusion. You have to know that they won't panic, won't scream, and won't start unloading their weapons until the other side has had a chance to extend its feelers to you. If you are unsure, remind yourself of how they reacted the last time they saw a spider. Family members are unlikely to be the best choice.

A change-oriented individual[21] who will be able to readily adjust to the extraterrestrial's psychology and influence other humans to adapt accordingly would help in the aftermath of the confrontation.

Ensure that there are no divisions within your entourage. Avoid the possibility that the extraterrestrial will exploit existing divisions as the Spanish conquistadors did to the Aztecs, through

---

[21] C. Boyce, *Extraterrestrial Encounter: A Personal Perspective*, New Jersey, Chartwell Books, 1979, p. 37.

the Aztecs' traditional enemy, the Indians of Tlaxcala.[22] For instance, don't be accompanied by your next-door neighbour if he has been pestering you to pull down that tree house you built for the kids. Next thing you know, he'll be ratting on you to the extraterrestrial about the bunker you built. You will then be deprived of a secret place to hide should the extraterrestrial be on the verge of overwhelming you.

When speaking to your companion, you don't want to be overheard by alien beings. Secure communications in the midst of an adversary can make all the difference to the outcome. It's best to use coded Navajo Native American language. It has been proven in wartime never to have been able to be cracked by enemy humans let alone aliens.[23] I'd start learning it now as it takes many years to master the inflections and tonal nuances. It has many words for one of our verbs depending on the noun it is relating to. However, if you are expecting a confrontation soon, it may be better to send two Navajo code talkers instead.

[22] D. Raybeck, 'Contact Considerations: A Cross-Cultural Perspective', in D. A. Vakoch (ed.), *Archaeology, Anthropology, and Interstellar Communication*, Washington DC, NASA, 2014, ch. 9, pp. 144-145.

[23] N. Aaseng, *Navajo Code Talkers*, 2nd edn., New York, Walker & Company, 2002, pp. 75, 104.

4.3 Personal case study

It wasn't so easy to get someone to accompany me. I got it into my head that the person I needed was the local zookeeper. She was a sprightly athletic-looking girl in her twenties. Her straight brown hair almost reached her waist. This is how the conversation went:

I spotted the zookeeper entering the tortoise enclosure with a bucket in hand. She shut the gate behind her.

'I like most animals, but there is one that I am apprehensive about,' I said, leaning over the fence.

'Oh,' she said while feeding the tortoises with her slender arms. Her silver bracelets slid up and down as she did.

'One of my clients' dogs came in by air. I'm not even sure that it is a dog, but I don't know what else it could be.'

'If you want to talk, the education centre is more than happy to discuss any animal topic you like. It is just past the dingoes we recently acquired from Australia.'

'No, wait, I'm looking for someone who understands animals, and you're reading the cues from all kinds of animals all day long.'

She stopped and looked up.

'I need your help in approaching this . . . dog. I was hoping you'd be able to tag along with me.'

'Look, the rounds I have to do are long enough without having to call on your home.'

'Think of the potential research opportunity it could open up for you! A dog like this doesn't appear just anywhere.'

She came out of the enclosure and closed the gate. Her hand was still clutching the ball of lettuce she was feeding the tortoises with. She looked me in the eye. 'I don't even know you.'

'Claude Joseph, dog washer, happy to make your acquaintance,' I said, holding out my detergent-bleached hand.

'Emily Watkins,' she replied nonchalantly, ignoring my hand.

'Here's a video recording of it. What do you think?' I asked, handing her my camera. I wondered how she would react to its bulging head, its protruding shoulders as if it wore a footballer's shoulder pads, and its dog-tailored jumpsuit. What would she think of it somersaulting in my children's sandpit or leaping in the air to fetch my parcel before the delivery drone reached my mailbox? To top it all off, I showed her a scene of it disembarking a spacecraft that even SpaceBiz would be in awe of. No matter that it was through a dog flap.

She looked stunned. 'OK, I'll go. Give me ten minutes to finish up here and I'll meet you at the turnstiles.'

I ambled to the zoo shop and bought some green frogs, red frogs, and various coloured snakes for my children—the candy kind, of course—to pass the time.

When Emily joined me, I noticed she had changed her boots. She was considerate enough not to stain my car floor from droppings she had trodden on throughout the day. The smell would surely have irritated Veronica. I also noticed the belt she wore with her shorts doubled up as a portable charging battery and had a couple of connectors hooked in.

'You're making good use of your charging belt,' I said.

'I like to keep my torch batteries topped up so I can check on the nocturnal animals. Total darkness freaks me out. Ever since I was locked in a storeroom one night as a child, I carry a torch. But it needs to be charged frequently, so I wear a charger. I don't know how people used to find room in their pockets for a portable phone charger as well as everything else they need to carry. Much better to have it built into your belt, which you have to wear anyway. It holds your pants up instead of dragging them down,' said Emily.

'Too right,' I replied.

'Fancy that animal wearing a costume. Must be some jetsetter's pampered pet,' she said as we walked to my car.

'From some exotic location he or she visited, no doubt,' I added.

'How did you come to be washing dogs?'

'I'm actually a qualified hairdresser. I don't think some of my customers from back when I ran a hair salon appreciated the extra effort I put into their hairstyling. Sure, they were as polite and courteous as when collecting their jacket-and-skirt ensemble from the dry cleaner's. But hairdressing is an artistic pursuit. I was contributing to the persona their circle would identify them by for the next month. Would it hurt to express some delight? I thought, if my efforts are not going to be appreciated, I may as well follow another pursuit.'

'Yeah, but why dogs?'

'Dogs,' I echoed. 'Dogs go about their day with gusto. They are simply barking glad to see you. Did you know that dogs can help you live longer just by being happy?'

'I can relate to that,' replied Emily.

After Emily stepped into my car, she reclined the seat back and shut her eyes. I empathised that traipsing around a zoo all day with bags of animal food and plant fertiliser would be tiring work.

I parked in my garage and reached for the whipper snipper leaning on the wall. It was the only long implement I could find to defend ourselves with.

The dog creature was in the backyard, watching the neighbour's cat climb a tree. Then it flicked its head towards us and gave out an almighty bellow. Its front paws pounded the lawn as it bounded towards us.

'Yikes!' exclaimed Emily.

I threw my whipper snipper at it. I wasn't going anywhere near it. We ran inside.

'Shut the door!' I yelled to Emily. 'Forgive me, that wasn't the introduction I intended.'

'Muzzle the creature or enclose it before it kills someone! An animal like that shouldn't be on the loose.'

'What sort of animal do you think it is?'

'An anomaly.'

Precaution 5

Demonstrate Goodwill

5.1 Advice

You should overtly demonstrate goodwill but only covertly be armed.

You have to keep in mind that studies[24] have shown that human beings are already biased to favour people that look like them or the people who surrounded them in childhood. This is even though a person of different appearance may actually have more in common with them. So, try not to be put off if the extraterrestrial looks repulsive to you. It may be looking repulsive simply because of its difference.

---

[24] M. Banaji and A. Greenwald, *Blind Spot: Hidden Biases of Good People,* trade paperback edn., New York, Bantam Books, 2016, pp. 126–127, 130.

Especially don't contort your face in a look of horror. It may already have self-esteem issues. If it is sensitive, your gaping may well offend the being, causing it to clam up.

I would only be hesitant if the creature were covered in body armour, whether that be biological or artificial.

You cannot discount the possibility that the extraterrestrial may be well-intentioned, so you have to start your encounter by showing goodwill.

I suggest serving a plate of sliced watermelon. Water is presumed to be the lifeblood of the universe, while the redness is bright and attractive like a gift should be. If the alien doesn't respond, eat a slice yourself to show that there is nothing wrong with it.

If the alien still doesn't respond, determine whether it is a robot. If you have seen other aliens and some look identical to each other, they are probably robots. Robots are generally built from a limited number of design templates to cut costs. I guess it would be a letdown if your much-anticipated confrontation turned out to be with a robot. Of course, it wouldn't be interested in any refreshment, but you could offer to oil its joints as a gesture of goodwill.

Showing goodwill is not a one-off process. Each time you meet, goodwill needs to be imparted. On a second confrontation, you may offer to patch up the heat shield on the extraterrestrial's spacecraft.

If you happen to be on a slope and it is shorter, stand on lower ground. Conversely, if it is taller, stand on higher ground. That will allow you to make the best and fairest eye contact.

Correct body language is crucial. Be relaxed, be open, and smile. Intelligent aliens are likely to have evolved over a very long time the ability to recognise universal expressions of fear, anxiety, hostility, and calm. Make eye contact with the alien when it grunts, to show your interest in its utterances. Slight variations in your facial expressions, when added to good eye contact, will convey that you are listening.

Unfortunately, specific gestures won't be so easy. Alien beings may use completely different gestures. There is a strong possibility of misinterpretation. So, don't pat an alien on the back, don't try and shake hands with it, don't wave to it, don't nod to it, don't even salute it. Forget about any sign language you may have learned at the deaf institute and forget about any charades you learned at those teenage party games nights. And don't use any symbol or icon. It could easily mean to it the opposite of what you intend.

Imagine that you were living in the seventeenth century and you saw a lone person talking to the air and gesticulating. You might be excused for thinking the person was unhinged. The centuries of development that made a mobile phone possible would be beyond your grasp. So, if the extraterrestrial is behaving like it stepped out of an Escher[25] artwork, don't expect to understand it. You cannot see the whole picture.

---

[25] M. Fellows, *The Life and Works of Escher*, Bristol, Great Britain, Parragon Book Service, 1995.

Interact with the extraterrestrial to answer the same sort of questions you would ask when making conversation with a person you just met.

Firstly, determine where it lives. Show the alien a star chart of our spiral arm[26] of the Milky Way galaxy, pointing to yourself and then to the star that denotes our sun. Then hand the star chart to the alien. If the alien is receptive, it will likewise point to itself and then some other star. Use that space pen that I suggested you bring to draw a circle around the star it indicated it came from. This information is vital for GovSnoop to know how long we can expect between visits and which direction in the sky to monitor.

Secondly, find whether it has come here before. Walk with the alien to where it is has set up its outdoor instruments alongside its spacecraft. If you can see a chamber for measuring atmospheric composition, then the extraterrestrial is on a maiden voyage. There would be no point in conducting that experiment a second time, and it would definitely be done on a first visit to Earth. It would show that the alien is merely on an exploratory mission rather than on an exploit.

Thirdly, see whether it wants to keep in touch. Give it a solar-powered satellite phone to keep. From a second satellite phone, send it an emoji and encourage it to reply. If you get a happy-looking emoji back, you have indeed succeeded in demonstrating goodwill. You will also have given it a means to contact you.

---

[26] Our sun is in the Orion Arm of the Milky Way galaxy. This minor arm is also known as the Orion Spur.

You may have come to know the alien's planetary anthem, either by overhearing a recital during a landing ceremony or through listening to a radio transmission. Play it back to the alien in a solemn manner to show you respect its customs. If you can't sing, bring along somebody who can. You don't want to offend it with a poor rendition.

You may have been fortunate enough to have been selected for an interstellar mission. Should you set foot on an inhabited planet, the worst thing you can do is plant your flag on it. That smacks of intent to colonise. Conversely, if the extraterrestrial plants a flag on our planet, that is a bad sign. I would inform GovSnoop at once.

Don't be surprised if the alien already knows a lot about us. If it starts quoting our hopes for world peace or flashing a photo of the London Eye,[27] it may be from Gliese. That's because on 9 October 2008, we transmitted a digital radio time capsule called 'A Message from Earth' to planet Gliese 581c, which is twenty light years away. It contained 501 selected text messages that included images.

If that's all the alien has received, then its knowledge would be dated. However, if the alien has been picking up radio transmissions and public broadcasts on its way here, it may well be aware of current news and entertainment. Hum the first line of the chorus from the latest pop hit. If it hums back the next line, then it may be more tuned in than some of your friends.

---

[27] A giant observation wheel on the south bank of the Thames River in London—a photo of the very slow Ferris wheel was transmitted to Gliese 581c.

When it comes to beverages, the alien may pour you a heady brew. As long as you have seen it drinking from a mug served from the same ceremonial bowl, take a sip so as not to offend it. I wouldn't swallow it though. Discreetly spit it out when nobody is watching. If you need to, create a diversion that enables you to do so. I find that using plants works best as they are good absorbers of fluid. Just come up to a plant in a delighted manner saying something like 'Oh, what a beautiful Venus flytrap,' then let loose down its funnel.

If you have demonstrated goodwill using the examples in this chapter but the extraterrestrial remains silent, what should you do? The silence may make you feel uncomfortable and make you think the extraterrestrial is suspicious. It may lead you to fill the gap it creates.[28]

I wouldn't fret. It could be mute, or it could be using a method of communication you are unable to detect. I doubt you have the necessary recording equipment to measure frequencies it may be emitting. That's all right; you can't carry everything with you.

However, don't think you can break its silence by making it laugh. Mimicking Aunt Thelma's skit at the club last week would not only be embarrassing, it wouldn't elicit one fleeting giggle from the alien. The closest any other animal on Earth gets to laughter

---

[28] C. Richards and F. Walsh, *Negotiating*, Canberra, Australian Government Publishing Service, 1990, pp. 33–34, 47, 53.

is a dog's gasp or a chimpanzee's panting.[29] Laughter is a human trait.

Just enjoy the shared silence together. Try and be in unison with the alien's posture and motion. When you feel cosmically fulfilled, slowly back away, facing it at all times until you are out of sight.

Finally, I know throughout history, humans have looked upon other animals as food. This book is titled *Confronting an Extraterrestrial*, not *Eating an Extraterrestrial*. It would be extremely bad form and show complete lack of goodwill if you were to slice it up and serve it to your family for dinner!

5.2 Personal case study

If my washing an extraterrestrial upon first contact wasn't showing goodwill, I don't know what is. I didn't really have a choice. At the time, I thought it may have been a made-to-order breed belonging to a very wealthy client. I couldn't afford to disappoint the client in front of the watching media.

Now I felt I had to counter the mongrel's ill will to Emily and me with kindness. After all, it could be suffering from separation anxiety. When we saw it snoozing on the back lawn, we ventured

---

[29] J. Askenasy, 'Laughter: Interdisciplinary View', *Israeli Journal for Humor Research*, issue 5, June 2014, p. 89.

out of the house to give Emily a closer look. She picked up a feather from the lawn.

The dog was lying on its back, spread eagled.

Emily toyed with the feather. 'I wonder whether it is ticklish.'

I couldn't tell whether she was serious or joking. 'Don't even try,' I warned. In any case, Emily had forgotten the feather, flicking it behind her. Now she was looming over the dog.

'It smells like a cross between cinnamon and shampoo,' she remarked.

'That's because I gave it a bath,' I explained.

'You washed it?' replied Emily in disbelief.

'I had to. It was the grand opening, and the media were filming.'

Emily mumbled, 'A bit extravagant.' She looked down at the animal. 'I've never seen any dog breed like it. It has the overall body shape of a dog, but its features and bone structure are all wrong. It looks like the result of a genetic engineering experiment gone haywire.'

Positioned like a frog, she sank her head to the level of the dog. She scrutinised its every angle and snapped photos. I was nervous that the infernal shutter sound of her camera would wake the dog up. 'There's a fold where the tail should be, like a modesty flap.' She turned towards its head and ever so gently touched the bristles on the dog's neck. As she did, I saw the pale orange ring around its neck. It looked like a life ring against its sea-blue costume.

'Someone has put an electronic band around the mutant's neck and fitted a camera to its forehead,' I said.

'I expect we're on interplanetary broadvision,' joked Emily, adjusting her brown hair. She had no idea how close to the truth she was.

'Well, we can't have that.' I tried removing the camera, but I couldn't without hurting the animal. 'I'll be back in a moment,' I said, slipping away. I returned with some masking tape, some meat loaf, and toys.

'This will have to serve as a lens cap,' I said as I wrapped the masking tape around the camera lens on its head.

'It makes its forehead look bandaged, as if it has been in a fight,' she remarked, making a droopy face.

I placed the meat loaf that I knew it liked in front of it so upon waking, it would be drawn to the smell. I scattered dog toys from my business across the lawn to entertain it.

'That's not the way to confront the dog especially after it chased us into the house. On the next encounter, you need to let it know who is boss, who is pack leader. You need to command respect and exude confidence by being calm and assertive. Pandering to its wants will declare you to be subservient, making it feel it holds the dominant status. Admittedly, I'm as much to blame for running away from it, but I was taken off guard. We have to start over and take control,' said Emily.

'How do you suggest we do that?'

'Start by making it sit down and stay down for five minutes. Then set rules, boundaries, and limitations and be consistent. Avoid direct eye contact, which the dog interprets as a challenge. Instead, appear aloof.'

I returned the meat loaf and toys to the house and came back.

'I'll show you how it is done, this time,' said Emily.

When the dog woke, Emily was already standing over it, firmly saying 'Sit' whenever it tried to rise.

When she moved away, it tried to get up.

'No, no, stop it, sit down,' she said, pointing closely at it.

She stood her ground.

The dog whimpered and stayed still as if it was beholden to Emily. I was impressed with how easily it worked.

The front door opened and out stepped Veronica wearing a tousled-wave hairdo.

'What is that stinking dog doing here?' she exclaimed.

'That's why I brought the zookeeper. This is Emily,' I said, trying to calm her down.

'Oh, good morning, Emily,' said Veronica cordially. She quickly turned back to me. 'Honestly, Claude, you need to call the exterminators, no kid will go near it in the zoo. I'm going to the Progress Association meeting. I don't want to see it when I get back.' She walked straight past a gleaming model of progress, the alien spaceship, without batting an eyelid.

I looked sheepishly at Emily. She gave me a sympathetic smile.

The space dog looked up and scurried towards the pile of memory plugs it had deposited in the empty garden pot. With its drooling mouth, it carried the pot towards the spacecraft and through the flap.

'Hoarding hound dog,' said Emily, delighted at its prowess.

'Either it is smart or it is well trained,' I replied.

Precaution 6

Do Not Board Their Spacecraft!

6.1 Danger of their spacecraft

There's a reason this chapter's title is punctuated by an exclamation mark.

I'm sure you've heard frightful stories of anal probes, brain scans, and body dissections. If your companion is of the opposite sex, the aliens are likely to want to dissect both of you to study the full complement of human organs. So, there'll be nobody to rescue you. If one of you is a woman, they may use you or her as a surrogate to give birth to some grotesque alien creature.

They may conduct any manner of experiments on you. Seeing how you respond to electric shock or withstand being rotated in a centrifuge[30] comes to mind.

At best, they'll shine their torch in your eye, jab you with sedatives, extract blood samples, and generally poke and prod in places you'd rather they not touch. You don't want to expose yourself to that! It will take a lifetime of therapy to get over it, if you survive.

Earth is where you want to stay. Honestly, there's no place better. Think of the blue skies, green meadows, and sandy beaches you'd be giving up. Think of all the loved ones you may never see again and all the live shows you may never watch. On their planet, they might not even have a pub!

Your body wouldn't be adapted to any other planet, no matter how habitable it is to the extraterrestrials. You would be a misfit.

Their spacecraft will be like a prison to you, worse than Alcatraz.[31] Instead of San Francisco Bay surrounding you, only the void of deep space will be outside. The artificial environment in their spacecraft is likely to be modelled on their own planet's atmosphere and gravity, which could be nothing like Earth's. You'll need inhalers, nasal tubing, and gravity braces just to survive. A

---

[30] By way of example, the United States Navy's Johnsville human centrifuge that subjected early astronauts to pull 32-G forces was referred to by *Time* magazine as a 'gruesome merry-go-round'.

[31] Alcatraz Island has an abandoned federal prison which held some of America's most notorious prisoners.

good indication of the difference will be how much breathing apparatus they are using to walk on our planet.

Flying saucers have been reported a staggering number of times around the world. Swiss psychiatrist and psychoanalyst Carl Jung attributed this to our collective psyche seeking the wholeness that the circle symbol provides.[32] So you may need to slap the shell of the landed saucer to make sure you weren't just seeing a vision. But go no further. Spinning saucers are a particularly troubling spacecraft. They are prone to make you dizzy even if it is only the outside shell that is rotating.

6.2 Resisting their spacecraft

Bright lights from a landed spacecraft can draw you in. They can have a mesmerising effect, especially if you drank too many cocktails at last night's Christmas party. You have to resist your urge to ascend those stairs they dropped down for you. Don't be like a moth drawn to the light. Shield your eyes with a visor. Turn around, for God's sake!

If they dangle in front of you an elixir of life and run their finger down their supple skin, don't believe them for a minute. They are probably wearing a fake skin so as not to scare you. Our

---

[32] C.G. Jung, *Flying Saucers: A Modern Myth of Things Seen in the Skies*, London, Routledge & Kegan Paul, 1959, pp. 33, 78.

own cosmetic manufacturers have been selling that promise for years without result.

Should they roll out a red carpet all the way into their spacecraft, don't even step on it. There might be super glue on it. They might pull it in like a lizard's tongue before you know what is happening. What you thought was a black-tie event could well hide a tie that chokes you.

If you have been lassoed and are being forcibly pulled into a spacecraft, dig your heels in. Remember those spiked soles I advised you to wear. They will help here. Or cut the elastic cord with your teeth or that pocketknife I told you to throw in. As extra incentive, think of the moment when the tension is released and the cord hits your alien abductor smack bang in his or her face.

However, the biggest pull will come from your own curiosity, and nobody can blame you for that. Exploration and discovery have been a hallmark of human endeavour. But achieve it a smarter way. Send in a remote-control camera in the form of a fly. Let it do your snooping while you watch from the safety of your parked car.

If the aliens have forced you to board their spaceship, get their commander's attention. Turn on that torch I suggested you bring and point the torchlight downwards. Use it to play-act a rocket lifting off, struggling to ascend, then crashing back down. That will fuel doubts that their mission planners would have accommodated the addition of your weight in the lift-off budget. So, unless they want to leave behind one of their wide-eyed star voyagers in exchange, they could be putting their whole crew in jeopardy. With any luck, they'll let you down.

6.3 Visitation via wormhole

If you have seen beings in the neighbourhood wearing spacesuits that are off the scale in size and not your basic human shape, then you have indeed found yourself a crew of visiting extraterrestrials. Should scouting around fail to uncover any spacecraft or landing module, I would be particularly concerned. Even more so if the alien astronauts were peering through a telescope focused on the night sky, as that would confirm they have no idea where they are, not having navigated themselves here.

What if the extraterrestrials didn't arrive via spaceship? What if giant beings from our nearest star system Alpha Centauri arrived via wormhole through a fold in space? Then the same restraint applies to a wormhole as it did to a spacecraft. Under no circumstances enter the wormhole, even if it is fronted by a dazzling psychedelic star gate.

The chances of a wormhole connecting two life-supporting planets together would be extremely slender. It is much more likely that the other end of the wormhole is deep space. That's why the aliens are wearing spacesuits. Do you really want to step through, with no friendly spaceship docked at the other end to greet you and shuttle you off to Alpha Centauri?

The best way of locating the entrance to the wormhole is to see where all the cave-dwelling bats are disappearing into. They are bound to be attracted to a tunnel opening. Listen for their piercing sound and wing rotating at dusk to find them heading off to roost. Keep looking up at their broad wings as you chase them on your motorbike until you see them swoop down and enter the wormhole. If they don't flock out at dawn to feed on insects, you know they have met adversity.

The heavy spacesuits of the aliens will slow them down. While you have the advantage, chase the shortcut-taking aliens back into the wormhole using kelpie dogs if necessary. Before you know it, millions of them might come sneaking through. Call on GovSnoop to immediately secure the border crossing and shut the flaming gate! You are way out of your depth in this situation.

6.4 Personal case study

The spaceship loomed in front of Emily and me.

'Let's go in,' said Emily with enthusiasm.

'Shouldn't we call GovSnoop first?'

'It's on your lawn,' she said.

'All right, but if it turns out to be extraterrestrial in origin, we'll need to wait for GovSnoop to explore further,' I said.

'Hmmm,' said Emily. I wasn't sure whether she agreed or not.

We looked for an entrance that would let more than a dog through. Emily located a circular door and felt with her fingers for a way of opening it. Her nerves made her cough. I think it triggered a voice-activated unit because the door suddenly slid up into a recess. It left a round opening that we could fit through. Stooping down, we quickly entered.

The odour of animal waste was unmistakable.

The interior was machine laden like you would expect an engine room to be. What space existed was shadowy and bleak. Only a square chamber and winding passage gave room for the dog to exercise.

Emily shone her torch in the darkened areas to make sure there was nothing lurking there. Suddenly she saw on the wall small indigo blue creatures scatter. She had disturbed the globular-shaped bugs feeding on the space dog's waste. She turned away in revulsion.

Putting her torch in her pocket, Emily looked at the pilot capsule where the dog must have sat. The seat was perfectly moulded for the dog. She ran her fingers across the smooth surface and noticed that the material was reshaping itself to the contours of her fingers. She moved her hand away as if she had been touching a snake. She looked back at me, aghast.

Now reluctant to touch surfaces, Emily stayed in the centre of the square chamber and looked around. I stepped onto the raised corner. Suddenly, a machine started shooting large plastic plates at Emily. One after another, they hit her. They only stopped when I stepped off the raised section. She gave me a look of admonishment when she realised it was me who triggered it.

Emily picked up a plate. 'Look at the mouth marks on the edge of the plate. It looks like the animal has been playing fetch.'

I saw that the machine that shot them out was stacked high with disks. 'Yes, and this exercise machine operates like a tennis-ball machine flinging disks at the user. Whenever the dog wanted to play, it must have stepped on the raised section and then leapt to fetch the disk mid-air in the zero-gravity environment.'

Out of nowhere, a short can-shaped cleaning robot scooted across the floor and collected all the disks. It extended its arm and inserted them back in the machine. It disappeared as quickly as it had come.

Feeling out of our comfort zone, we exited the spaceship.

'That was no genetically modified dog. It's extraterrestrial just like the seat and the spacecraft. Why send a dog?' asked Emily.

I could only think of the Soviet space program. I remembered reading about the adulation the USSR[33] people had for their heroic space dogs. People felt affection and compassion for them. The canines were pioneers for humanity, chosen for their obedience, hardiness, and endurance, not to mention photogenic attributes. They were featured on every postage stamp, every postcard, every matchbox.

'As a test flight just like we did, I mean the Soviet Union launched several dogs into orbit. This one at least appears to have fared better than Laika, the first Soviet dog in orbit, who died a few hours after launch,'[34] I said.

'Yeah, but this dog has been sent to another planet. Why not send a wheeled contraption?' she asked.

---

[33] Former Union of Soviet Socialist Republics

[34] O. Turkina, *Soviet Space Dogs*, London, FUEL Design & Publishing, 2014, pp. 29, 89.

'Because a dog is ideal. That's why SpaceBiz called the contraptions they sent to investigate Mars rovers, a dog's name.[35] They were emulating a dog. Why shouldn't the aliens send a real dog to Earth? We have a life-supporting planet with oxygen and water, unlike Mars. Moreover, Earth has a cluttered surface. It's full of bushes and man-made obstacles that a vehicle would have difficulty negotiating.'

'You have a point,' she acknowledged. 'Those blue creatures must have been extraterrestrial too.'

'They must have been deliberately put on board to perform natural waste management. In the zero-gravity environment, some of the dung would end up sticking to the walls of the spacecraft. You need a creature to scrape it off the walls and turn it into a form that is easier for the spacecraft to vacuum-suck into space.'

'You mean like dung beetles? I often see them in the zoo, rolling dung into round balls.'

'That's right. But did you know dung beetles use the Milky Way as a single guidepost to orient and navigate themselves along straight paths?'[36]

'Incredible. They would have been more fitting co-travellers for the space dog,' remarked Emily.

---

[35] M. Hardin, 'New Mars rover FIDO works like a dog', *Universe, Jet Propulsion Laboratory*, vol. 29, no. 10, May 14, 1999, pp. 1, 4.

[36] M. Dacke, E. Baird, M. Byrne, C.H. Scholtz, and E.J. Warrant, 'Dung Beetles Use the Milky Way for Orientation', *Current Biology*, vol. 23, issue 4, 18 February 2013, pp. 298–300.

'What do you suggest we do with the dog?' I asked.

'Trap it and put it in the zoo, in a non-public enclosure where it will be out of harm's way.' I liked her thinking. I was glad I chose a zookeeper to accompany me.

● ● ●

We arranged to meet the GovSnoop agents at my house. I wore my Italian jacket and pressed trousers for the event. A congregation of birds invited themselves and chirped from my magnolia trees.

The day started fine, but a severe storm was brewing. I hoped my shampoo supplies would be delivered before the storm hit. Otherwise, the delivery drone might take a dive before it got here.

Emily had arrived early, wearing her sandy-coloured zoo uniform. Her hair was tied back in a long ponytail. I had a chance to chat.

'I'm so glad you could return,' I said, smiling.

However, she seemed anxious. 'Are you sure only a dog came out of the spacecraft? I may be able to handle a dog or bear-like creature, but I wouldn't want to confront its master.'

'I haven't seen anybody else,' I said. 'And you saw there was no seating for them in the spacecraft.'

'I guess I'm just a little jittery. Do you run your dog wash all on your own?' she asked.

'Yes, my wife will step in if she has to but she really hates the smell of dogs. She tends to overdo the amount of shampoo she uses. Mrs Crompton's collie came out with a voluminous frizz, having had its natural oils stripped out by the excessive shampoo. However, if my business takes off, I am prepared to hire assistants.'

I wanted to show Emily the operation of my dog wash business in case her dingoes could use a bath.

'Would you like me to show you around my dog wash?'

'Yes, I'm curious to see how you cater for pups.'

First, I showed her the drive-through from the front of the property to the rear lane at the back of the property. The automobile automatic sensing gate at the front let driverless cars through so long as there were no dogs on the inside, trying to escape. I let her examine my assortment of pup harnesses that I offer clients for use in their driverless vehicles. I also had towels, combs, and brushes for sale.

I showed off the renovation I did to my laundry, which now occupies the full-length side of the house alongside the drive-through. I pointed out the parallel high-gauge pipes I had the plumber put in to serve the multiple hoses in the sinks. You could wash a schoolyard of uniforms if you needed to. I turned on the spa jets to demonstrate the force of the bubbles I could generate. The whole property was fenced in so that I wouldn't lose any dogs. A tall sign out the front read, 'Claude's Dog Wash.'

My phone rang. It was Sophie Redrup.

'Excuse me a moment,' I said to Emily. 'Hi, Sophie. What can I do for you?' I asked.

'Mum wants Terence to be sent back early today. She heard there was going to be a storm.'

'Will do. How did you go at your debating competition?'

'Just lost, I'm afraid,' she replied.

'Maybe next time,' I said and hung up.

'Let me show you how I wash the dogs,' I said, turning back to Emily.

I led Mrs Redrup's white-and-tan fox terrier from her car.

'My, you certainly are a smart-looking dog,' I said, seeing how trim and alert he looked.

'Arf!'

'Aww, look at his tail go!' said Emily.

I patted Terence on his back and placed him in one of the sinks.

'Shall I close the car door?' offered Emily.

'No need,' I said.

I gave Terence a general bath and rinse using what was left of my hypoallergenic shampoo.

'I've ordered a full range of shampoo supplies. They should be delivered today,' I said, feeling my shelf looked bare.

'Ooh,' said Emily, stepping back when Terence rose suddenly, splashing water on her uniform.

'Sorry,' I said, passing her a towel.

'At least it's clean water,' she replied. 'Not like the hippo pond.'

I pointed to the shelf. 'There is the extra-sensitive shampoo bottle that I would have used for a pup.'

Emily picked up the bottle and smiled at the picture of a cute basset pup half closing its eye.

I proceeded to give Terence a medicated bath and rinse, using scent-removal shampoo.

'I can see brightness and colour coming to his coat, and he smells divine,' said Emily.

I paid special attention to cleaning his ears. First, I shook a bottle of ear relief wash that is alcohol-free and non-stinging. Then I massaged the base of his ears and distributed the solution into his ear canals.

Finishing off, I applied moisturiser to his short flat coat.

'Could be useful for the dingo pups in the petting area,' said Emily. 'Even though they are purebred desert dingoes, they are no less affectionate than your regular dog. The children love holding and stroking them.'

We heard the vibration of a motor vehicle. A black van with a parabolic dish antenna on the roof pulled up on the street. Two Native American Navajos inside were wearing radiation suits. They stepped out and passed two spare suits to us. They each held a rifle.

Emily stared at the rifles. She feared they might be used on the space dog.

'Don't worry, they are only precautionary,' said one of the agents to placate her.

I let Terence down to have the run of the house. He shook his body and sped off.

'Good morning, I'm Emily from Watch Your Fingers Zoo.'

'I can see that safety is a core value of your zoo,' remarked agent LoRenzo.

Emily smiled back as she donned her radiation suit.

'And I'm Claude, I wash dogs.' LoRenzo gave me a dismissive look.

I felt that I needed to get a better name for my dog wash.

'Agents LoRenzo and Manuelito,' said LoRenzo. It was hard to see their faces through their radiation headgear. They looked like astronauts on our own planet.

LoRenzo and Manuelito looked up at the spacecraft as if assessing in their minds the threat it posed.

'We found a door on the side,' said Emily, trying to be helpful.

'You've been inside?' Manuelito asked, raising his eyebrow.

'We didn't know it was extraterrestrial. We just had a peek,' I explained.

'What's it like inside?'

'Creepy,' said Emily.

She tried a short cough to open the door like before. Manuelito looked baffled when it worked.

The agents were very cautious about entering it. They peered in a few times before finally lowering their heads and entering. They were worried about more than their fingers.

When we were inside, I saw the pot load of memory plugs the space dog had pinched from me. It was planning to take back data from Earth.

I pointed to the pot. 'Those are mine. Don't worry. They are only cat videos.'

Emily chuckled. 'They'll think Earth is Planet of the Cats.'

'If they do, it will serve them right for sending us one of their dogs,' I replied.

The pot of memory plugs was not as significant in itself as the expectations it raised about the bowl of large buttons beside it.

'These don't belong to me,' I said to be clear.

I picked one of the buttons up. It felt polished and pliant. I pressed it with my thumb. It didn't have a connector like my memory plugs; it didn't need one. All on its own, it projected an image of what appeared to be an inventory record of a machine of unknown purpose, judging by the ordered symbols overlaying the image. I pressed the button again, and a schematic was displayed.

'This space dog is looking more and more like a spy dog,' I said.

'I wonder which machine-fabricating civilisation the spy dog stole these memory buttons from?' said LoRenzo.

Manuelito wasn't going to wonder. Looking like he hit the jackpot, he scooped up the buttons like they were casino chips and dropped them into his deep pocket.

There were no computer screens or instrument panels as the spacecraft wasn't manned by intelligent beings. Instead there were various food and drink dispensers and air-conditioning systems to keep the dog alive. There was the comfortable seat capsule where the dog was encouraged to sleep.

A robotic arm hung high above the harness with a nozzle and brush at the end. I pondered for a moment what it was for.

'Ah, an automated dry cleaner for the space dog. I should get one of those for the dog wash.'

I reached for the nozzle and peered in. A residual powder akin to baking soda sprayed the window of my helmet.

'Touch the seat,' suggested Emily to the agents, not wanting to demonstrate it herself.

The animated sensation made them quickly retract their fingers. Emily smirked when she watched that.

'Careful, don't step on the raised section,' I warned Manuelito. He stepped back just in time, almost bumping into the sleek computer system that occupied the corner.

LoRenzo was busy digitising the spacecraft in three dimensions with a scanner. What better way to show his director the spacecraft than through a virtual tour?

An awful growl echoed through the spacecraft. We all looked down. The space dog poked its sandy head through the flap. The band around its neck started flashing orange light. The same orange colour flashed at the same rate on a panel on the computer system beside Manuelito.

The GovSnoop agents started talking in Navajo code.

'What are you saying?' I asked, baffled.

Agent LoRenzo scrawled on a piece of paper while cupping his other hand around the paper. He folded it and handed it to me. I unfolded it, cupping my hands around it, without knowing why I needed to. I read what it said.

> We're in an alien spacecraft that could potentially be monitored by an on-board artificial intelligence unit. We can't risk being understood. So, we have to revert to the tried and proven Navajo code that was so successful during World War II. What I said was 'It's a proximity

reader.' The spacecraft computer detected the instant that the dog was back in range.

Not wanting to be left out of the loop, Emily did the same.

Suddenly the door closed and gas started being released from a manifold. Emily looked at me. Her face went ghost white. A terrible thought crossed her mind. It was enough to make her hair curl. She tried coughing vigorously but it wouldn't open the door from the inside.

The spacecraft energised with a jolt. A loud hum that turned into a rumble came from the back of the spacecraft.

I peered out a porthole and saw my trees shaking and leaves swirling around in an updraft. I knew we shouldn't have boarded their spacecraft. But Emily was relieved when she realised that the purpose of the gas was only to pressurise the spacecraft not to poison us.

'It's going to blast off!' I said to Emily.

'No, I thought it was hungry lions stowed on board.'

I looked back to see her teasing expression. I wasn't used to being mocked.

'Well, don't just stand there,' said Emily, turning around. 'The proximity band . . . Chuck it out of the dog flap!' she demanded, pointing to the dog.

'Why?'

'You read the note. We need to make the system think the dog is no longer on board. The blast-off sequence has to be aborted. Unclip it from the dog now!'

Then I understood what Emily was getting at. The spacecraft must have been preprogrammed to return to its home planet once the dog was safely back inside after a preset amount of time. I reached for the dog's neck then swiftly retracted my hand. 'I can't. The dog is trying to bite me.'

'Let me try.' She distracted the dog with one hand while reaching for its orange collar with the other. The collar had no buckle; it was tamper-proof.

I later learned that the proximity reader collar on the space dog was more than that; it was a homing device for the space dog to find its way back to the spaceship.

I pointed to the GovSnoop agents. 'They may have a plan.' I hoped.

The GovSnoop agents were conversing in Navajo code. We had no idea what they were saying but we heard low tones, high tones, rising tones, and falling tones. They didn't have a plan but it didn't matter anyway.

The more they talked, the more the spacecraft's lighting momentarily dimmed. You could hear the computer rapidly clicking like an old telephone exchange while its indicator lights flickered in unison. The cooling fans went into overdrive, expelling heat generated by the central processers. The artificial intelligence unit was skipping computer cycles dedicated to on-board maintenance in order to crack the Navajo code. It had given itself an impossible challenge. It was going into overload and neglecting its environmental and housekeeping duties. Even its launch sequence was stalled.

Every now and then, the door momentarily opened a small amount. The gap was just high enough for a person to duck through.

'That's our chance,' I said, pointing to the door. I waved to the Navajos to get their attention. 'Let's get out of here!' The Navajos paused their speech. I panicked, 'Keep talking!'

I had always thought of small talk as having no consequence. Never had I thought it could save my life.

'Chase the dog through when it opens,' said Emily. 'We need to study it.'

Each time the door partially opened, one person darted through until we all made it outside, including the dog.

The spacecraft abandoned its launch sequence and de-energised. My ears popped and my heart stopped racing.

'What a relief!' I said. 'Never again will I board an alien spacecraft.'

Epilogue

In my garden, all that remained of the chorus of birds was a solo orange-breasted robin that had ignored the rumble and fumes from the spacecraft. We unzipped our radiation suits, folded them up, and returned them to the van.

Now I could see LoRenzo and Manuelito's high cheekbones. They both wore blue denim pants and heavy shoes. Manuelito's outfit was complemented by a bright turquoise headband.

It was time to restrain the space dog.

'I'll get my dog trap,' said Emily.

Emily drove her 'Watch Your Fingers Zoo' branded ute behind Mrs Redrup's car in the drive-through. She lifted the cage off the back and set it down. She deposited some fresh chicken within to entice the dog and then set the cage door to snap shut upon entry.

'I've got just the enclosure for it in the zoo. You will be able to spend as much time as you like, examining it there,' said Emily to the GovSnoop agents.

'Appreciate the offer,' said LoRenzo. 'However, we'll need to arrange transfer to the National Biological Laboratory.[37] We need to study its biology.'

'Oh, I was hoping to run it through a training and assessment exercise.' She tensed. 'They won't harm it, will they?'

'No lasting harm,' replied LoRenzo.

Emily gave him a piercing look. She coaxed the dog to enter the cage. Maybe it didn't like chicken. Going through her mind was the dieting regime she would have to put this animal through. Going through my mind was relief that this alien encounter was coming to an end for me.

But it wasn't to be. Leaping towards me, the space dog scooped up my camera strap in its jaws and ran off. It was familiar with cameras, having had one clasped to its head.

'Get the dog! The dog!' I screamed.

I ran so fast I thought my legs were going to fall off. Emily kept alongside me without even losing her breath. She had experience chasing zoo animals around their enclosure. We ran three laps around the house. But the space dog seemed to have vanished.

An ear-wrenching clunk broke the silence. A metallic object had hit the top of my dog-wash extension and, after reverberating loudly, stuck fast to it. It was close to the wind turbine on the roof of the drive-through.

'What on Earth is that?' asked Emily.

---

[37] International Biological Threat Reduction division of Sandia National Laboratories, Albuquerque, New Mexico

LoRenzo and Manuelito peered at it and then conversed in Navajo. Although I couldn't understand a word they were saying, I could see the excited looks they gave each other. They took photos of it and reported back to their headquarters. They seemed to be more interested in it than the spacecraft or the dog.

'Can you stop talking Navajo? What are you saying?' I asked.

'Come into our van. It's soundproof,' offered LoRenzo.

We all piled into the van. It was nice. It was decked out with curtains, a bar, and some high-tech monitoring equipment. We huddled together on the leather seating.

'Would you like something to drink?' asked Manuelito.

'Not the time for it,' I said. 'You seem to know what landed on the roof.'

'Yes, it's a Matter Splatter Mark 2,' said LoRenzo, spitting the words out.

'Forgive my ignorance, but what is a Matter Splatter?' I asked.

Manuelito was quick to elucidate. 'Well, a Mark 1 model landed on a Florida golf course two days ago. An amateur golfer retrieving a wayward ball stumbled on it. The course now has a nineteenth hole with the hapless golfer buried two feet underneath. It's a bomb.'

'A bomb!' exclaimed Emily.

'Which is on my dog wash!' I reminded the others. 'I only just completed the renovation. It cost me a tidy sum.'

'What's so special about a Mark 2?' enquired Emily, narrowing her eyes.

'You can see this one has an antenna. The Florida one didn't. That makes it a tracking drone until it explodes,' said LoRenzo.

I thought for a moment. 'That could be a problem. Like the Mars rovers, I think the space dog could be transmitting whatever its camera records, which is presently the inside of my makeshift lens cap. You don't think the drone followed the dog here by locking on to its transmission?'

'Let's check whether the space dog is transmitting.' LoRenzo pressed a few buttons to activate the parabolic dish on the roof. 'Well, what do you know! There is currently a transmission from your house, and it's an auditory signal. You capped its lens, but you didn't muffle its microphone.'

'Where is it transmitting to?' I asked.

'It is beaming towards . . . Sirius in the Canis Major constellation—the Dog Star!'

We couldn't contain our laughter.

Knowing for sure that the space dog was still around, I left the van to resume searching for it. I went straight to my dog wash since that was under the tracking drone. It had to be close. I had only started looking for the space dog when I heard Veronica chasing the terrier out of our living room.

'Why is this terrier inside our house? I told you to keep the dog wash door closed. The dog is making all our carpets smell.'

'Sorry,' I replied.

To tell you the truth, I had forgotten that he was still inside. I ran a terry towel over his fur to soak up any remaining moisture. I had left Mrs Redrup's front car door open from when I had carried it out. So, I just hollered for the terrier to get back on board. The terrier scampered in. I buckled the dog up so the car security system would register that it was wearing a seatbelt. I set the destination, enabled the self-drive, and shut the door. As the car pulled away, I noticed the space dog crouching on the floor of the back seat, still with my camera.

Suddenly, I heard a thundering roar from the roof of the dog wash. I didn't know which way I should look.

I called to LoRenzo, 'It was in the car,' but LoRenzo's eyes were fixed on the tracking drone.

I turned in time to see the tracking drone disengage itself from my roof and zoom in the direction of Mrs Redrup's car.

'The space dog is in the car,' I repeated.

'I'm more concerned about that tracking drone,' said LoRenzo, lining up his rifle with one of its four rotors.

He fired at the rotor, being careful not to hit the bomb compartment. The quietness of the neighbourhood was punctured by the sound of gunshot. Veronica lifted up the kitchen window to see what happened, while the neighbour's cat hid under a parked car.

The tracking drone tipped at one end and started to fall. It quickly re-stabilised itself by adjusting the speed of its remaining three rotors to compensate.

'What about Mrs Redrup's car? Shall we give chase?' I asked.

'How would we stop the car? It's not like we have a tyre-shredding spike strip that we can throw across the road ahead of it,' said LoRenzo.

'What about executing a PIT[38] manoeuvre to spin the car out of control like the police do?' suggested Manuelito. His exuberance was like that of a simulation pilot about to play space fighter.

'Absolutely not! We cannot put so much as a blemish on my customer's car,' I insisted.

'Can you tell me your client's address?'

I rattled off Mrs Redrup's street address. I caught a glint in his eye.

'Calling headquarters to check if there are agents in the vicinity of Mrs Redrup's house,' said LoRenzo, digits hitting digits. His head looked downwards as he spoke on the phone. I thought he was trying to ascertain what variety of lawn I had laid down. I knew the neighbours were envious of it. You know what they say, 'The grass is always greener . . .'

He looked up. 'Good news: they'll have two agents waiting in front of her house for when her car returns.'

'Wouldn't those agents be too petrified to hold the space dog in their van, what with a Matter Splatter Mark 2 tracking it?' I asked.

'It's OK, our vans are Faraday cages. They won't just keep the dog in, they'll keep its electromagnetic transmission in too. Besides, I've slowed down that tracking drone,' said LoRenzo. I liked his confidence.

---

[38] Precision Immobilisation Technique to bump a fleeing car on the side to make it spin out as developed by Fairfax County Police Department, Virginia, United States

'Just lock that spaceship up. We're heading back to base before the parcel storm hits,' said Manuelito.

'Me too,' said Emily. 'I've got zoo enclosures to batten down. Toodle-oo.'

I nodded and went to my shed to find a padlock to use. Once I locked the spaceship, I headed to my house.

The familiar sound of rotors spinning caught my attention. I was pleased to see a drone safely delivering my shampoo supplies to my mailbox in time. I carried them into my extended laundry and arranged them by scent, from fruity to flowery. I found the bigger dogs like lemon scent, while the poodles prefer frangipani.

I decided my new business name needed to be more upmarket. I toyed with a few names and once I settled on one, placed an order for promotional T-shirts. I would leave a complimentary shirt in each customer's driverless car.

A nagging feeling that I had forgotten something made me go over the day's events. Then I remembered my camera being snatched by the space dog. I hadn't checked whether my video recordings of the space dog had streamed successfully to my home computer. If they hadn't, that meant I would have lost my record of the encounter. I flung open my study door and took my monitor out of sleep mode. The file-receiving app in the corner of my desktop had hung two days ago. 'Damn!' I thought.

I pondered why the Matter Splatter Mark 2 didn't explode over the hiding dog while it was motionless in Mrs Redrup's car. I realised that was because one of my wind turbines was installed on the roof of the drive-through, shielding Mrs Redrup's car underneath. Mrs Redrup was lucky that I had installed that wind turbine where I did. It saved both her terrier and her car from an instant splattering.

I sank into the couch and watched a rerun of a broadvision show. I was blissfully unaware of what would be going down in court in the coming days.

● ● ●

It wasn't until late in the evening that I plucked up enough courage to ring Mrs Redrup to check that her terrier arrived home safely. I knew she was protective of her dog and fastidious over his well-being. I wasn't prepared for how furious and accusatory she was.

'Terence arrived home late and traumatised. I can't believe you let a vicious-looking dog into my car. And do you think it is funny playing cat videos to Terence? I was waiting all afternoon for my car to return. Why did it arrive so late when I specifically had Sophie instruct you to return it early? I was powerless to save my daughter from the parcel storm. If it wasn't for that same rogue dog catching a parcel drone mid-air, my daughter might have been severely injured.'

'I am very sorry. I had no idea the dog was in your car until I saw it leave.' I tried to console her. 'Lucky it saved your daughter from being hit, though.'

'Is that all you can say? How could you even think that I should be grateful?' she snapped. 'I would have already picked up

Sophie if my car hadn't been delayed from your dog wash. You were supposed to leave my car door closed while washing Terence. If you had done so, the rogue dog couldn't have got in the back seat, and my terrier wouldn't have been traumatised.'

'As soon as I saw the rogue dog was in your car, I arranged for GovSnoop to capture it on arrival at your house.'

Then I heard her burst into tears. 'Worst of all, a bomb exploded on top of the GovSnoop van parked on the street. My front garden is now in ruins.'

Now I was in shock. I started to tremble. 'Is the driver OK?'

'Yes, nobody was in the van at the time.'

'Phew,' I uttered in relief. 'I'm sorry for all that has happened. Can I make it up to you?'

'You will in court.'

• • •

The following details are what my attorney ascertained from both the prosecution and GovSnoop during his preparation of my defence in Mrs Redrup's civil litigation against me.

Mrs Redrup had been fretting. Her daughter hadn't yet walked home from school. She was afraid she'd get caught in the parcel storm that the weather channel warned was coming her way. She felt frustrated because she couldn't pick her up because the driverless car was late from the dog wash. Why was it taking it so long? She should have got more referrals before choosing that dog washer.

The weather channel had kept telling everyone to shelter indoors. Just like a tornado blows man-made things about, a storm front is able to blow off course already airborne parcel-carrying drones. But unlike tornado debris that is spun about, these all come in the same direction, in force. Especially the long-distance mail that was sent before the storm warning. They called it mail hail.

Mrs Redrup was waiting for her driverless car. Every so often, she drew her curtain to see if it was back in her driveway. What she didn't know at the time was that there was an additional occupant on board who wasn't wearing a seatbelt. When the driverless car detected the occupant wasn't buckled, it capped its speed very low for safety. Also, because some driverless cars never get driven by a person, they need to make their own way to a car wash every so often. Taking full advantage of that, a motorway-operated car wash enticed it to be washed that afternoon.

All of a sudden, Mrs Redrup heard shouting outside. She saw two men rush out of their vans. They flung open the rear doors of one of the vans. At long last, her cleaner-than-expected car had pulled up in the driveway. Before she was able to step out of her house to bring her bathed fox terrier inside, the two men surrounded the car with a large net. Oddly, they opened the back door. She frowned; the terrier was in the front. They threw a net over the unusual dog and carried the wrestling animal to the van that had the back open.

The two men shut the rear doors of the van and walked up to Mrs Redrup's front door and knocked. They had seen her peeking through the curtain.

'We are from GovSnoop. Forgive us for our unannounced visit and entering your car. It was only to capture the rogue animal that had snuck inside. You shouldn't encounter any more disturbance. We will be leaving now. Have a nice evening.'

'You too, good to see the government helping out with vicious dogs. Have a safe trip back.'

At that moment, the impaired tracking drone arrived. It had followed the space dog all the way from my house but struggled to match even the severely capped speed of the driverless car. The three heard a loud clunk as the drone grappled the top of the van that was holding the space dog. It carried a metallic block with lenses on three sides. Steam seemed to be emitted from a matrix of openings. It looked eerie in the fading light.

The GovSnoop agents couldn't understand how the tracking drone had detected the space dog's transmissions with all the shielding their van was enclosed in. Mrs Redrup was astounded at the amount of attention her property was receiving.

Within seconds, the tracking drone exploded, destroying the van entirely, splitting open her terrier's favourite oak tree and cracking up her birdbath sculpture. She and the two agents were stunned senseless by the ear-shattering sound. They looked in horror at the raging ball of fire consuming the van. LoRenzo and Manuelito felt the fragility of their lives having been spared by nothing more than fortuitous timing.

The GovSnoop agents later assumed that the space dog was vaporised in the blast because forensic examination found no trace of it. Their private thoughts were that the space dog must have done something diabolical to earn the wrath of alien beings.

Considering that the tracking drone did detect the space dog's transmissions and that Mrs Redrup told me she had subsequently seen the space dog, I presumed the agent must have left the driver door ajar. It would have not only broken the electromagnetic shielding of the vehicle, it would have allowed the space dog to escape out the front.

Although dazed by this incident, Mrs Redrup hadn't forgotten her terrier and her daughter. She hurried down her driveway and opened her front passenger car door. She unbuckled her beloved fox terrier and carried him to the safety of her home, closing the door behind him.

Mrs Redrup ran back to her car as the wind hit. She struggled to open the driver's door as the force of the wind was pushing it back. She squeezed in before it slammed shut. Annoying cat videos were playing inside. Her finger jabbed the off button. She frantically followed the path she knew her daughter took to go to school and return from. The route was in the direction the storm was blowing.

The rain pelted down on her windscreen, blurring her vision while the wind buffeted her car. She could make out her daughter in the distance walking hurriedly towards her, holding her leather schoolbag over her head. Her strawberry-blonde hair was flattened over her face by the wind. Mrs Redrup wept in relief. Moments later, this was replaced by horror as she saw a large parcel drone toppling down towards her daughter.

Mrs Redrup omitted to mention to her attorney what happened next, but she had already told me on the phone. Miraculously, the same bear-like animal that she had seen the agents trap leapt in the air as if it were weightless and caught the parcel drone in its snout. It barrelled along the ground, eventually coming to a halt. Unbeknown to Mrs Redrup, it was a space dog doing its acrobatic routine. It was part of its exercise regime in the zero-gravity chamber of its spacecraft for most of the journey to Earth.

Mrs Redrup's car screeched to a stop beside her daughter. Sophie heaved the door open against the force of the wind and collapsed onto the front passenger seat before any other drones came. Her wet schoolbag was dripping over her legs. It was impossible to tell what ran down her face: rainwater or tears. Her mother, paranoid by the bizarre day, drove twice as slowly, determined to make it home safely.

Coming back to her conventional suburban neighbourhood, she saw the full extent of the bomb crater in her front garden.

● ● ●

'Ladies and gentlemen of the jury, I intend to prove that the defendant wilfully set about to cause anguish to the plaintiff. Satellite records,' the prosecutor cited, 'indicate that a tracking drone holding a bomb came from the defendant's house and exploded at the front of the plaintiff's property. What was the defendant doing with a bomb?' The implication was that it was mine.

'Moreover, the plaintiff's car returned very late from the defendant's dog wash with a vicious-looking bear-like dog in the back seat.'

When it was my attorney's turn to make his opening statement, he countered, 'The same satellite records show that sometime later the drone was at the plaintiff's house. Does that make the ownership transfer to her?'

The gallery jeered.

'Order, please,' demanded the judge turning to the gallery momentarily. 'Continue.'

'As for the lateness of the plaintiff's car, it wasn't all my client's fault. E-Tag motorway billing records showed that the driverless car succumbed to marketing messages on the return journey, encouraging it to enter a car wash affiliated to the motorway operators. I will hold that the defendant could have no possible motive for causing trauma to his own client or her dog.'

'I call Claude Joseph to the stand,' said the judge.

I took my position and looked over the gallery. I was surprised at how many people were interested in my case. The proportion of women in the courtroom was quite high. I wondered how many had read the article on my business launch in *Women's Circle* magazine.

Veronica was there holding a picture of an elephant to keep my spirits up. It was from the flash cards she used to teach our children with. If it looked like I was going to be facing damages, she was going to bring up the elephant in the room, the great big alien spaceship docked in our yard. My attorney didn't want to mention it, GovSnoop didn't want to mention it, and the prosecution wouldn't mention it even though it could be seen in the corner of a photograph from the women's magazine they would display on the large courtroom screen.

I appreciated her resolve, but we agreed that she should only use it as a last resort as I didn't want to get on the wrong side of GovSnoop if I could avoid it.

'You may begin your questioning,' said the judge.

'Could you explain to the court how a tracking bomb happened to be at your house?' asked the prosecutor.

'It landed on the roof of my dog wash all on its own. It is a drone, after all. I had nothing to do with it,' I said honestly.

My attorney had advised me beforehand not to bring up what GovSnoop told me about the drone unless they were prepared to corroborate. Otherwise, the credibility of my testimony would be challenged. What the court was not privy to was the GovSnoop classified file on the case: that it was an alien tracking drone from another planet to that of the space dog. It was sent to kill the space dog.

The prosecutor had dug into my Internet viewing habits. 'Service provider records that we subpoenaed show that you have spent considerable time viewing cat videos. As an operator of a dog wash, it brings your loyalty towards your clients' dogs into question. How do you explain that conflict in interest?'

'I just find their antics amusing, especially kittens,' I maintained.

Giggles erupted.

'Another outburst like that from the gallery and I'll have this courtroom cleared!' The judge eyeballed those in the second row. 'You may continue questioning the defendant.'

'Mrs Redrup found a cat video playing in her car when she rescued Terence. It was of a rancher trying to herd a hundred cats. She noticed an unfamiliar memory plug inserted in her car entertainment system console. Why would you insert a memory plug of cat videos into your client's car and set it to play?'

'I didn't.'

'Isn't the memory plug yours?'

'Yes, but that doesn't mean I put it there.'

'Well, who do you expect us to believe put it there, the rogue dog?' That is precisely what I believed, but I couldn't say so.

The gallery was about to laugh but swiftly buttoned its lips.

'Mrs Redrup's home surveillance video footage confirmed GovSnoop had two vehicles parked out the front of her house. She said she saw two agents step out and remove a vicious-looking dog from the back seat of her car when it returned from the defendant's dog wash. This has been corroborated by GovSnoop.'

The judge then spoke. 'I have to advise the court that the GovSnoop agents who captured the unsightly dog were unable to attend court today. However, they left a statement that I will read to you now: "Our only involvement was to capture and remove a rogue dog. It is part of the community service we perform. We had stayed in our vans a considerable time because the driverless car that we were waiting for took so long to arrive."'

The smoking gun, however, was the exclusive in *Women's Circle* on my dog-wash launch. The prosecution displayed photographs from the magazine on the large courtroom monitor. The pictures clearly showed me leading the unrestrained bear-like dog to my laundry two days before the incident.

'Don't you screen the dogs you allow onto your property?' the prosecutor asked.

'It didn't occur to me. If nothing else, the scoop proves that I am fair and caring in my treatment of all dogs,' I countered.

'Mrs Redrup's self-drive car log showed its computer announced, "Would the back-seat passenger please buckle up. Safety law requires speed reduction to be applied whilst any passenger remains unbuckled. Invoking speed reduction now. Your journey time estimate has been recalculated to be two hours and seven minutes." The log further showed the computer began to electronically display in big bright letters on the rear window, "Speed capped" to elicit understanding from any driver who may be behind. Could you explain to the jury why you let the rogue dog into my client's car, unbuckled?'

'As I have told Mrs Redrup on the phone, I had no idea the dog was in her car until I saw it depart. It was I who called on GovSnoop to capture it.'

'I have no further questions, Your Honour.'

'I understand the plaintiff is seeking damages,' said the judge. 'Can the prosecution outline what for?'

'Firstly, damage to her property from the bomb blast. It tore up half of her front garden. My client's home insurer wouldn't cover the repair cost of her birdbath sculpture because although their policy includes improvements such as fixed water features, it doesn't cover damage caused by an act intended to cause damage.' He glared at me as he said that. 'Neither would it cover removal of her oak tree and landscape restoration works.'

The judge interjected. 'It should be noted that a GovSnoop van was also destroyed in the blast. However, they are not seeking damages.'

'Secondly, trauma to her terrier. I call Mr Shrinkler to the stand as a hardship case witness.'

'What is your occupation?'

'A dog psychologist. I was brought in by Mrs Redrup to treat Terence after the incident.'

'Can you give the court your assessment of how Terence has been impacted by the events of that afternoon?' asked the prosecutor.

'The dog has become withdrawn and housebound. He appears to be inconsolable. Worst of all, he won't enter the car anymore. Not after having been trapped with the vicious-looking dog while cat videos were playing.'

Mrs Redrup cringed at the reminder.

'What actions have you tried?'

'First, I vacuum-cleaned the back seat from fur that the bear-like animal shed and sand grains that it left behind. Then I opened the windows and sprayed deodoriser and air freshener, but still Terence wouldn't jump in. I even set up a small portable set of stairs to make it easier to climb into the car, but the terrier wouldn't budge. I tempted him with food and commanded him but nothing worked.'

'I have no further questions, Your Honour.'

'Court is now adjourned,' announced the judge.

● ● ●

I had no evidence to tender of the lead-up to the incident because the space dog lost my camera and my camera-to-home-computer streaming failed to operate. That's why you should always have someone check from time to time that it is operating.

After GovSnoop read transcripts of the first day's hearing they revised their position. As the explosion occurred on GovSnoop's watch, which is not something GovSnoop do lightly, they took some responsibility. Best of all, they privately settled with Mrs Redrup on my behalf. The truth was, they just wanted the court case to discontinue. The less that was aired about the tracking drone, the better. Jolly good of them to bail me out, I thought. That's why it pays to follow Precaution 1: Have GovSnoop Authority.

GovSnoop also allowed me to review their file on the matter to ensure it was consistent with my experience. Their conclusion was that the alien beings who sent the tracking drone were the primary reason for the space dog being on Earth in the first place. The dog was a decoy to divert the alien beings' attention away from the dog's planet onto ours. The decoy worked because the alien beings wanted to prevent the space dog from disseminating the information in the memory buttons it had pinched from them. Those buttons recorded technologies that they wanted to keep secret.

The spaceship had first landed on a dog-friendly golf course in Florida. Scared off by a Matter Splatter Mark 1 explosion, the space dog reboarded its spaceship, which then blasted off. Once high enough, the artificial intelligence unit of the spaceship used remote imaging to pinpoint another dog-friendly place. From space, it detected the shape of a dog, which it considered to be a good sign. That was the flower bed in my garden modelled on a dog. No wonder it skidded down to my dog wash!

My promotional T-shirts with a new business name had arrived—Show Dog Cleansing Spa. I was folding them when Manuelito rang. He was over the moon.

'You know what we found on one of those buttons?'

'Blueprints of a time machine,' I guessed.

'No, the design of a robot that is as powerful as any fictional superhero. That's why the tracking drone was after it, to stop other civilisations from copying their super bots. We'll be able to use them to fight crime and carry out rescues!'

'And watch their zip cord shoot out an anchor line to the tallest building,' I imagined.

'I'm serious, emergency help will never be the same again. They will be an unbeatable asset.'

'That's until the bad guys get hold of one,' I replied. 'We would do well to keep it secret too.' But there was no containing

Manuelito's excitement. He was already envisaging a brigade of them.

The phone call reminded me of the space dog. It may have been beastly, but the idea of sending a doglike animal into outer space intrigued me.

I was captivated by the Soviet Union's idolisation of their intrepid space dogs. Even though the space dogs came from the alleyways of Moscow, they revered them more than any show dog. A monument of Laika was erected in Moscow in 2008. It features a dog standing atop an abstract space rocket near a military research facility where staff had readied Laika for the flight.

The Soviet people felt deep sadness for Laika when they learned that she had not survived the journey. Then I thought of the space dog's interplanetary keepers. How much would they mourn if their space dog didn't return? How much would they celebrate if it did? I had no idea where it was. The last reported sighting was from Sophie's phone call.

'Terence won't be coming anymore,' Sophie informed me softly.

'I thought as much,' I replied. 'Your mother is still pretty mad at me, isn't she?'

'Yes, but I have to tell you, the most incredible thing happened!' she said.

'I'm listening.'

'When I was returning home from school during the storm, this bear-like dog leapt out of nowhere. Mum said it caught a parcel drone that was going to flatten my head. The next thing I knew, it was splayed on the ground with the rotor assembly still hanging out of its mouth.'

'Yes, your mum was saying,' I said.

'I thought it must have knocked itself out, the way it was just lying there. But on sports day, when our bus coach was cruising down the motorway, I saw it in the breakdown lane, still wearing its light-blue costume. It was head down, pacing like it was on a mission.'

'That was my customer,' I said, smiling.

'You're kidding.'

I was feeling disappointed to have lost Terence as a customer. However, my spirits were lifted when a driverless 'Watch Your Fingers Zoo' vehicle pulled up in my drive-through. Inside was a dingo pup with a note that read, 'Please wash me gently' with a smiley pup face underneath. I was thrilled at having gained the patronage of such an established business as the local zoo. Now I had a zoo as well as a pop star as a customer. The only thing that could have made it better was if the vehicle wasn't driverless. I had taken a liking to the zookeeper.

That wasn't the biggest surprise though. A week after the Redrup incident, the signage installers erected my new billboard, 'Show Dog Cleansing Spa'. As they were reversing out the front driveway, who should sneak into my front yard but the untiring space dog? The auto-sensing gate was only designed to prevent dogs from escaping, not entering.

I was flabbergasted at how far it must have trotted. It was then that I realised the proximity reader collar on the space dog was a homing device to the spacecraft.

The space dog sauntered across my lawn like it was on its home turf. It gulped some water from my lawn sprinkler head and entered the spacecraft through the dog flap. Within minutes, the spacecraft blasted off. The space dog's interplanetary keepers were going to celebrate!

Index